BIOGRAPHY OF
HAROLD WILSON

The Life and Legacy of Britain's Visionary Labour Prime Minister (1964-1970, 1974-1976)

Blake Hayden

Table of Contents

PART ONE

Childhood and Political Origins

In the quiet hamlet of Huddersfield, Harold Wilson started his road toward becoming one of Britain's most prominent Prime Ministers.

Wilson, who was born on March 11, 1916, grew up in a poor household and was surrounded by West Yorkshire's attractive surroundings.

His mother, Ethel Seddon Wilson, devoted her life to raising Harold and his siblings while his father, James Herbert Wilson, worked in the chemical industry.

Despite not being wealthy, the Wilson home was full of books and a sense of intellectual curiosity.

Early indications of Harold's intellectual prowess and sharp mind were evident. At the adjacent Royds Hall Grammar School, where he was a student, his academic aptitude began to stand out.

Wilson's interest in politics originally took root in this rural community.

He devoured newspapers as an adolescent and kept up with the tumultuous political events of the 1930s, such as the Great Depression and the ascent of Adolf Hitler in Germany.

These international occurrences had a significant influence on his worldview and sparked his determination to use politics to change the course of the world.

Wilson attended the University of Oxford to pursue his academic interests in philosophy, politics, and economics (PPE). His time at Oxford had a significant impact on him.

He developed his oratory talents and participated in heated discussions on political ideologies, socialism, and the function of the state in society.

During his stay at Oxford, he was also exposed to important philosophers who would later play crucial roles in British politics, such as Sir Isaiah Berlin and Sir Anthony Eden.

Wilson had a strong foundation in economics and political philosophy thanks to his schooling, which helped him become a powerful politician in the future.

The Post-War Political Landscape

Wilson's generation suffered a great deal as a result of the start of World War II in 1939. During this turbulent time, he thought it was his responsibility to serve his country rather than pursue a career in academics.

He entered the civil service and worked as a statistician, aiding in the planning of post-war rebuilding and analyzing economic statistics to support the war effort.

Wilson was made aware of the difficulties of leading a country at war and the complexity of governance during the war. His dedication to social justice and the well-being of the British people increased throughout this period.

Wilson's involvement in the war had a lasting impact on his political views and gave him important insights into the function of the government under pressure.

Britain confronted new difficulties as World War II came to an end.

Economic hardship, the necessity for rebuilding, and the fall of the British Empire were the hallmarks of the post-war period. Wilson kept a close eye on these events and saw the need for imaginative and daring strategies to rebuild the country and deal with the socioeconomic injustices that had existed for years.

The Labour Party was developing as a powerful force for change in the changing political environment.

Wilson identified strongly with Labour's principles of social justice and equality and saw them as how he might accomplish significant changes and influence the course of British history.

Wilson's swift ascension inside the Labour Party served as a signpost for his entrance into active politics. His academic rigor set him apart from his contemporaries thanks to his eloquence.

He soon found himself at the center of political talks and policy discussions, arguing for liberal ideas that appealed to a populace that was ready for change.

His early involvement with the Labour Party served as a springboard for his subsequent leadership positions.

The Road to 10 Downing Street

Wilson's ascent to power would be aided by his ability to relate to a variety of Labour members and his dedication to maintaining party cohesion.

Harold Wilson's trip to 10 Downing Street, the British Prime Minister's official home, was evidence of his political savvy and tenacity.

Wilson faced tough competition from inside the Labour Party, but his leadership skills shined through, and he progressively rose to the party levels.

His rise to the position of prime minister was characterized by fortitude, vision, and a strong desire to make life better for regular Britons.

He also brought with him a special combination of intellectual rigor, political savviness, and a resolve to implement progressive changes that would influence the future of Britain when he assumed the position of Prime Minister.

PART TWO

Taking the Lead

In October 1964, Harold Wilson became the country's prime minister, ushering in a new era in British politics.

His first time in office was characterized by a spirit of regeneration and hope. Wilson brought a new perspective to the position as the country's youngest prime minister in over a century, aiming to modernize and improve it.

Addressing the country's economic problems, which included a balance of payments crisis and inflationary pressures, was one of his first tasks.

Wilson's administration lost little time in putting into effect several economic measures designed to stabilize the economy and safeguard the interests of the working class.

It was a challenging exercise of balance that would ultimately characterize his leadership style.

The "Swinging Sixties," a period of social transformation, creative creativity, and a transforming cultural environment, occurred during Wilson's first term. Carnaby Street in London and the Beatles were at the vanguard of this revolution in Britain.

Wilson's administration supported this cultural transition because they understood how crucial it was to keep in touch with the hopes and wishes of the younger generation.

Wilson's Leadership Style

Wilson tried to portray Britain as a contemporary, progressive country at this time, and the "white heat of technology" and the promise of a brighter future were major themes.

Harold Wilson was known for his pragmatic leadership style and dedication to reaching compromise.

He appreciated the opinions of his Cabinet colleagues and believed in the strength of a team effort. He had a wide range of personalities and abilities in his cabinet, including Roy Jenkins, Barbara Castle, and Denis Healey, all of whom were crucial in determining the course of government policy.

Wilson's aptitude for juggling conflicting interests within the Labour Party was shown by his ability to lead a lively and sometimes contentious Cabinet.

His ability to listen, adapt, and find common ground in his leadership style suited him well throughout his tenure as prime minister.

The administration dealt with ongoing economic difficulties notwithstanding the optimism of the 1960s. A key point in his first tenure was the 1967 sterling crisis. A devaluation brought on by speculative assaults on the pound rocked the British economy's trust.

Wilson's handling of the situation was a crisis management masterpiece. Devaluation, according to him, was required to increase exports and bring back economic stability.

Despite being a contentious political choice, it eventually served to stabilize the British economy and pave the way for a period of steady prosperity.

Harold Wilson's focus on innovation and technical progress is one of his lasting legacies. In his well-known description of the 1960s as a "white heat" of technical change, he underscored the need for Britain to adopt new technology to stay competitive in the world arena.

Wilson's administration made significant investments in science and technology, education, and R&D during his first term.

His dedication to knowledge and advancement is shown by the founding of the Open University, which aims to increase access to higher education.

The Vietnam War, a war that sharply divided the world community, defined the 1960s.

Wilson had to strike a difficult balance between maintaining the "special relationship" with the United States and dealing with the growing anti-war sentiment in Britain.

PART THREE

Reforms and Policies

Harold Wilson's dedication to social reforms and the growth of the welfare state was one of his most notable accomplishments as prime minister.

Wilson's administration aimed to establish a society that was fairer and more egalitarian by building on the principles set out by the post-war Labour government.

His revolutionary initiatives while he was in power, such as greater financial assistance for families, enhanced accessibility to social housing, and the expansion of benefits to those in need.

These initiatives attempted to reduce poverty and provide vulnerable residents with a safety net.

Wilson's background and early experiences in Huddersfield, where he saw the sufferings of working-class families during the Great Depression, were the foundation of his commitment to social justice.

He made it his goal as prime minister to correct these injustices and enhance the standard of living for average Britons.

Wilson's vision for a contemporary and progressive Britain was built on the foundation of education. He thought that everyone should have the opportunity to get a high-quality education. To do this, his administration introduced several educational reforms that altered the nation's educational system.

The Open University was established in 1969, leaving one of Wilson's educational contributions that has endured the longest.

This cutting-edge college sought to provide those who had lost out on regular university education chances for higher education.

Numerous people looking to further their knowledge and skills were given access to higher education thanks to the Open University's flexible approach to learning and remote education.

Healthcare Reforms and the National Health Service

The National Health Service (NHS) served as a pillar of post-war Britain, and Wilson's administration continued to fund and develop this crucial organization.

Healthcare delivery in the NHS significantly improved under his direction, with new medical technology being used and services being increased.

Wilson was dedicated to improving healthcare outside of the NHS. His administration introduced healthcare reforms with the goals of lowering health disparities, enhancing maternity and child health, and improving mental health services.

These changes represented Wilson's conviction that a robust and successful country depends on a healthy populace.

The National Plan

The "National Plan," a comprehensive economic plan intended to modernize British industry, increase productivity, and foster economic development, was at the center of Wilson's economic agenda.

It included a range of challenging goals for spending, R&D, and employment.

Wilson's administration aimed to maximize the potential of crucial sectors including industry, technology, and aerospace via the National Plan.

The strategy was supported by a dedication to regional development, with an emphasis on reducing the economic gaps in the nation's various regions.

Urban Planning and Housing

In the 1960s, there was a severe housing crisis in Britain, affecting a large number of residents. To combat this situation, Wilson's administration launched significant housing and urban planning programs.

Wilson's government worked to make sure that everyone had a safe place to live via extensive housing development projects and urban revitalization initiatives.

In addition to addressing the housing deficit, the objective was to build thriving, living communities for families.

Britain's demographics saw dramatic changes in the 1960s, partly as a result of immigration from former colonies.

Wilson's administration had to deal with the complicated problem of racial relations as a result of the inflow of immigrants, which presented both possibilities and problems for British society.

The government's attitude to immigration and the measures adopted to encourage social integration and fight prejudice are also covered in this chapter. It explores the Race Relations Act of 1965, which sought to end racial discrimination in public services, employment, and housing.

Harold Wilson's attempts to resolve racial and ethnic difficulties were a reflection of his dedication to promoting an inclusive and peaceful society.

In the decades that followed, a more varied and tolerant Britain was made possible by the policies of his administration.

PART FOUR

International Affairs

During the time that Harold Wilson served as prime minister, there were important possibilities and difficulties on the international stage.

The "special relationship" between the United Kingdom and the United States was at the core of his foreign strategy. Wilson understood the significance of this partnership in influencing global affairs and furthering British interests.

Wilson negotiated difficult diplomatic terrain with American presidents like Lyndon B. Johnson and Richard Nixon when he was in office. He was crucial in promoting collaboration on matters like nuclear disarmament and the Vietnam War and reconciling transatlantic conflicts.

Wilson's diplomatic skill and dedication to the special relationship demonstrated his awareness of how the world was changing and the need for strategic alliances in an interconnected society.

Africa underwent independence in the 1960s and 1970s, and the Rhodesian Crisis presented a serious obstacle for Wilson's administration.

In 1965, Rhodesia, led by Ian Smith, unilaterally proclaimed its independence from Britain, breaking both international law and the rule of majority.

Wilson's response to the Rhodesian conflict was determined by his dedication to the advancement of democratic administration and decolonization.

To end the conflict and facilitate a smooth transition to majority rule in Rhodesia, his administration tried diplomatic measures, sanctions, and dialogue.

Wilson's commitment to supporting the concepts of self-determination and decolonization while managing the difficulties of international diplomacy was highlighted by the Rhodesian problem.

Middle East Diplomacy and the Six-Day War

Wilson's administration faced a diplomatic challenge in the Middle East's 1967 Six-Day War.

Israel's battle with its Arab neighbors has repercussions throughout the globe and the region. Wilson aimed to contribute positively to solving the problem and fostering peace.

His administration backed resolutions from the UN Security Council requesting a halt to hostilities and a withdrawal of troops.

Harold Wilson was also aware of the need to keep Middle East diplomacy balanced and respect the rights and ambitions of both Israelis and Palestinians.

The Six-Day War emphasized Wilson's commitment to global peace and security while highlighting the difficulties and prospects of British foreign policy in the troubled Middle East.

The Conflicts in Northern Ireland

Wilson's administration had serious difficulties as a result of the Troubles in Northern Ireland, a lengthy period of sectarian bloodshed and political unrest.

Finding a solution to the issue was difficult since it had complicated political underpinnings and profound historical origins.

Wilson was dedicated to upholding law and order, safeguarding the unity between Northern Ireland and the rest of the UK, and promoting communication between various groups.

Although his administration received criticism from several sources, it aimed to strike a compromise between the need for security and the imperative of political advancement.

Wilson had ongoing difficulties with the Troubles in Northern Ireland, which would influence British politics for many years to come.

Wilson's Approach to the European Communities

The way Harold Wilson saw the European Communities (EC) was a reflection of how the dynamics of British-European relations were changing.

When Britain submitted its application for EC membership in 1967, he presided over a crucial turning moment during his first term.

His attempts to gain membership, nevertheless, were met with political obstacles and criticism from his party.

Wilson approached the EC with a pragmatist mindset. He accepted the financial advantages of entering the Common Market but also the need to defend British sovereignty and national interests.

The 1975 referendum, in which the British people chose to stay in the EC, was the culmination of his government's discussions with European allies.

Harold Wilson's handling of the EC matter demonstrated his capacity to steer clear of difficult discussions while upholding the democratic decision of the British people.

The Pound's Devaluation

Wilson's leadership at this crucial juncture was characterized by difficult choices and economic difficulties.

The administration took the challenging decision to weaken the currency in response to a crisis in the balance of payments and pressure on the pound's exchange rate. Despite opposition and political reaction, devaluation eventually aided in the restoration of economic stability and competitiveness.

His dedication to making difficult financial decisions for the long-term good of the British economy was emphasized by the move to devalue the pound. It was an illustration of his pragmatic and flexible leadership approach in the face of adversity.

PART FIVE

The Second Term

The political resurgence of Harold Wilson in 1974 was amazing. Following his first tenure as Prime Minister, Wilson briefly served in opposition before leading the Labour Party to victory in the general election of February 1974.

Wilson was asked to create a minority administration since this election produced a hung parliament.

He exhibited a feeling of continuity upon his return to 10 Downing Street, as well as a reinvigorated dedication to his goals for Britain.

He had to contend with a difficult political environment, a country undergoing social transition, and unpredictable economic conditions.

However, Wilson's leadership and expertise would be essential in surviving the turbulent years to come.

Economic difficulties during Harold Wilson's second tenure as premier would go on to characterize the time. Stagflation, a phenomenon that combined high inflation and slow economic development, plagued the 1970s and confronted policymakers with a special set of challenges.

A series of strikes and labor conflicts during the "Winter of Discontent" in 1978–1979 immobilized the nation.

Wilson's Political Legacy and Resignation

Public services were suspended, and the country had to deal with the fallout from these industrial activities. Wilson's administration was under intense pressure to reestablish stability and order in the British economy.

Harold Wilson unexpectedly announced in March 1976 that he would be resigning as prime minister and leader of the Labour Party.

His resignation, which was often attributed to health issues and other personal considerations, signaled the end of an era in British politics.

Wilson's departure paved the way for James Callaghan to succeed him, who took on the lingering political unrest and economic hardships of the late 1970s. Wilson, though, continued to participate in political discussions and stayed involved in politics as a backbencher.

The political legacy and management style of Harold Wilson are still the topic of discussion and evaluation.

The difficulties Wilson had throughout his two stints in office are taken into consideration when evaluating his reputation as a pragmatic and flexible leader.

His aptitude for navigating tricky political terrain, maintaining party cohesion, and interacting with global challenges is assessed.

Harold Wilson's administration's policies and reforms had a long-lasting effect on British society.

Harold Wilson's effect on British political theory and practice continued even after he gave up active politics.

Wilson's impact may be observed in later political leaders, from his dedication to social justice and welfare reforms to his pragmatism in foreign affairs. His influence on the Labour Party and the larger political scene evaluated, demonstrating the contributions' continuing value.

PART SIX

The Labour Party and Beyond

The Labour Party underwent a sea change when Harold Wilson retired from active politics. This chapter examines what happened following his resignation and how the party went about finding a new leader.

Wilson was followed by James Callaghan as prime minister and head of the Labour Party, and he took on the difficult issues of social upheaval and economic turbulence.

The Callaghan premiership, sometimes known as Callaghan's administration, struggled with the same economic issues that afflicted Wilson's second term.

The Labour Party and British politics are still influenced by the "Wilsonism" school of thought.

Wilson's foreign policy strategy, the Open University, healthcare reforms, and other programs are examined for their long-term effects.

Wilsonism's influence may be observed in succeeding Labour administrations, which have carried on his mission to create a more equitable and inclusive Britain.

Harold Wilson remained the Member of Parliament for Huyton after leaving his position as prime minister up to his departure from parliament in 1983.

Wilson's Retirement and Later Years

Wilson, a renowned senior statesman, continued to participate in public discourse and make contributions on a variety of topics.

In his retirement, he was able to engage in more personal activities like writing and speaking, providing a window into a man whose life had been mostly devoted to public service.

A distinct perspective on the person behind the political figure is provided by the memories and personal experiences shared by friends, coworkers, and family members. These individual viewpoints provide light on Wilson's personality, humor, and the human aspect of a politician who made significant contributions to British politics.

They depict a guy who was not just an accomplished politician but also a devoted spouse, caring parent, and devoted friend.

As we draw to a close, we consider Harold Wilson's continuing impact on the United Kingdom. His influence continued long after he left office, influencing the political, social, and economic climate of the country.

Wilson's influence on contemporary Britain is enormous, from the development of social assistance to his part in establishing the European Communities. His management of change and catastrophe showed the value of flexibility, pragmatism, and a dedication to social justice.